# Herb Gardening Made Easy

**How to plant and grow a delicious variety of herbs at home!**

# Table of Contents

Introduction ........................................................... iv

Chapter 1 – Why Grow Herbs ................................. 1

Chapter 2 – Growing Herbs at Home .................... 4

Chapter 3 – Best Culinary Herbs to Grow at Home
............................................................................... 9

Chapter 4 – Getting Rid of Pests Naturally ......... 24

Conclusion .......................................................... 26

# Introduction

I want to thank you and congratulate you for downloading the book, *"Herb Gardening Made Easy"*.

This book contains helpful information about herb gardening, and how you easily can begin your own herb garden at home.

You will soon discover the different herb varieties that you can grow, and what conditions they grow best in. This book is aimed at starting an herb garden at home, and includes suggestions for growing herbs inside your kitchen.

Herbs are delicious when fresh, and are great in meals compared to the preserved versions that you may buy. Not only are they handy for cooking, but many of them also produce pleasant aromas. Growing herbs indoors is not only beneficial for cooking, it can also be fun and rewarding!

This book will provide you the steps and strategies required to successfully grow a delicious variety of herbs, all from the comfort of your home! This book also includes a section on how to naturally keep your herbs free from pests and disease.

Gardening is a great hobby, and herb gardening is a perfect place to start, particularly if you have limited space. So, what are you waiting for? Read on to learn how you too can grow delicious herbs from home!

Thanks again for downloading this book, I hope you enjoy it!

# Chapter 1 – Why Grow Herbs

Having fresh herbs in the kitchen is quite helpful especially if you're the one trying to whip up the next flavorful dinner in the house. Fresh herbs serve as such a nice addition to any meal, but there is actually more to herbs than just adding flavor. Herbs also add nutritional value to your recipes. Some herbs are also medicinal. There are also herbs that are used for producing perfumes and scents.

*What's an Herb?*

Most people think of culinary herbs when you ask them about herbs. Well, generally speaking there are different types of herbs, and culinary herbs are usually at the forefront. Simply put, an herb is any plant that is used as food, for making perfume, useful as medicine, or used for flavoring other foods. In some parts of the world, herbs also have a certain spiritual significance in the lives of the people who use them.

Different parts of an herb can be put to good use. The leaves are usually the really flavorsome part of these plants. Other than the leaves, the roots, berries, stalks, and fruits can also be used depending on the particular herb.

*Culinary Herbs*

Culinary herbs are the ones that everyone uses to add flavor to food. Some may be occasionally confused for vegetables, but they're not. In fact, most of the time people only add just a pinch or a comparably small amount of herbs in a recipe. In contrast, vegetables and other ingredients usually take up the bulk of any recipe. Culinary herbs on the other hand are merely used to enhance the taste, aroma, and/or flavor of a dish.

*Medicinal Herbs*

Some herbs contain nutrients that are beneficial to man's health. Some culinary herbs can also be used as part of a treatment for disease. Do note that some herbs should only be consumed in small quantities. There are herbs that can become toxic if you consume too much. For instance, there are herbs that can be used to treat depression (such as St John's Wort). However, consuming too much will lead to a rather toxic overload on the body's systems; so some precaution should be taken.

*Other Benefits of Having Herbs at Home*

From what we have gathered so far we know that herbs make our food taste great and they can help with everyday aches and pains. Herbs also make our kitchens and the rest of our homes smell great. Some herbs are aromatic and they add a fresh, soothing scent.

You also save some money since you no longer have to buy herbs and spices from the store. What's more is that you actually get your herbs fresh instead of the dried or packaged ones.

Herbs also make homes look greener and more in touch with nature. Some herbs actually help soothe nerves and boost brain power. Caring for these little plants also help some people get some much needed stress relief.

Now that we've seen how beneficial herbs can be, in the next chapter we'll go over the steps on how to actually grow herbs at home.

# Chapter 2 – Growing Herbs at Home

Culinary herbs are perhaps the most popular type of herbs in the world. When you mention thyme, basil, oregano, or rosemary, people will almost immediately know that you're talking about herbs. Culinary herbs are the ones that you usually find in stores. You can find them dried and packed or you can order them fresh.

It's really easy to notice that fresh herbs have more flavor. They make your food tastier. Some cooking shows on TV even have the chef pinch off some herbs fresh from a live plant in a pot right inside the kitchen. If that idea has ever crossed your minds then the tips and tricks you'll find below will be very useful.

The good thing about culinary herbs is that you can incorporate them into any existing garden without any hassle. Some herbs are invasive, but most of them are very easy to manage. If you don't have a garden and all you can work with is a small bit of space in your apartment, then you can just grow your herbs in pots. Growing culinary herbs at home is just like growing any type of vegetable.

> ***HERB GROWING TIP:*** When you grow culinary herbs in small spaces or indoors, remember to harvest them at the peak of their flavor. There are herbs that give off a bitter flavor when they have passed their prime. You should also be careful when

choosing the type of fertilizer to use. Make sure that you check the label carefully and that the fertilizer you're using is made for edible plants.

*Growing Your Culinary Herbs Indoors*

If you're new to growing herbs indoors (culinary or medicinal) then start with annual herbs. Many of these types of herbs are sold cheap and you can usually start them from seeds.

Other than the type of plant you're going to start with, another thing you should be careful with is the potting soil you're going to use. Gardening suppliers often have rich potting soil on sale. Many of these packaged soils are well drained. If you have some gardening experience under your belt then you can make your own soil for your pots and make sure that they are well-drained.

Another issue that usually occurs when you plant culinary herbs at home is the use of pesticides and fertilizer. Some gardeners don't like to use fertilizer on the plants they're going to eat. However, if you're going to grow your culinary herbs in pots or containers, the amount of nutrients they can absorb will be very limited.

That is why adding some fertilizer to the pot soil is some sort of a standard practice for most gardeners. It's okay to use fertilizer; just make sure it's organic and it is supposed to be used for edible plants. Another important point that should be made here is that you shouldn't go crazy with fertilizer use. Remember that fertilizers (even the organic ones) are only supplements. They are meant to add nutrition to plants; they're not the main plant food.

Best practice (and a lot of experience) says that fertilizer use should be limited to every two weeks. You don't want to overuse your fertilizers even if you're using an all-purpose one or even if you dilute it with water.

> **REMINDER:** Over fertilizing may affect the way your herbs produce essential oils. These naturally produced oils are the things that give flavor to your food. Notice that if you over fertilize, your herbs tend to be less flavorsome. They won't smell as great or taste as great as they used to.

Other than limiting the use of fertilizer, you should also limit the use of pesticides. And if you're growing your culinary herbs indoors, they are less susceptible to disease and pests. Inside, you're also growing them in pots, which makes them easier to control and manage. There is an entire section in this book that provides alternative methods of pest control.

*Growing Medicinal Herbs*

You basically grow medicinal herbs the same way grow culinary herbs. In fact some culinary herbs are also medicinal in nature. They all need the same amount of care from their owners. You also need to give them some sun, water, and fertilizer. The same best practices and tips mentioned here for culinary herbs also applies to medicinal herbs.

## Starting Your Own Herb Garden at Home

The first thing you should do when you start your own herb garden at home is to decide which herbs you want to have. Make sure to grow only the herbs that you will actually use. There's no point in growing an herb you won't cook or use as medicine.

The next thing you should think about is where you want to grow them. You'll find a list of herbs in the next chapter and information about how to grow them properly. You must figure out how much sun each herb needs, how dry (or moist) their soil should be, and which plants you should grow side by side.

Herbs that require more sun include cilantro, chamomile, fennel, oregano, garlic, and basil. Herbs that can live in the shade include dill, mint, parsley, sage, and chives.

> ***TIP:*** Keep dill and fennel away from one another. They usually cross pollinate and end up producing some weird tasting seeds.

The taller herbs in your garden include rosemary, fennel, and dill. On the other hand, the shorter ones include parsley, oregano, mint, and thyme. The taller ones require larger pots than the shorter ones.

Now it's time for you to buy pots, potting soil, and young plants or starts from a garden supplier. Make sure to get soil that is blended especially for pots and containers. Fill the pot with potting soil. Your starts or young herbs will be growing with peat moss, which you will need to break up before you transplant into the pot. Make some room in the center of the pot, place the herb in the soil with the peat moss and then cover it with more garden soil. Remove some of the peat moss on the edge to prevent over dryness of the soil.

Now that you have them in pots you should place them where they can get as much sun as possible (about 6 hours a day, minimum). If you're growing them indoors, keep the herbs near the windows (especially windows that are facing east). Make sure that the room (i.e. your kitchen) is well lit.

Water your herbs according to how much they need. You can add an all-purpose liquid fertilizer, but you should rotate the use after every couple of weeks. Make sure to use organic fertilizer. Always use a diluted solution so you won't over fertilize the soil.

# Chapter 3 – Best Culinary Herbs to Grow at Home

The following are some of the best culinary herbs to grow at home. Some of them are best grown indoors while others are best grown outdoors. The key is the amount of sunlight that your herbs will get. Some herbs need more sunlight than others. The ones that don't require as much sunlight are the ones that you can grow successfully indoors.

**Growing Your Own Basil**

If you like Italian food then you should have some basil in the house. Basil is a staple in Italian cuisine, even though this culinary herb actually hails all the way from India. This herb is very aromatic and you will use the leaves in particular for your home cooking.

Basil leaves have a slightly minty taste. Well, the herb actually belongs to the mint family (which partially explains the minty taste). You will also notice the slight hint of a lemony taste as well.

Many folks grow their basils as annuals. They keep them growing until the sign of the first frost of the year comes along. They are best grown as perennials in places within zone 10 of the USDA hardiness zones. However, if you grow your basil indoors you have a chance to raise them as perennials as well.

*Sunlight Exposure*

Basil is best grown outdoors since they usually require a lot of sunlight. A lot of gardeners will recommend that you grow these herbs in areas where there is full sun. These are the optimal conditions for this herb (remember where they originated?) If grown optimally then you'll encounter fewer diseases with your basil and they will tend to be much sturdier.

If you intend to grow basil indoors you should place them near windows, even in a well lit room. They will require at least 6 hours of sunlight per day. If you have a porch, some sunny space in your garage, or some other area in your apartment where there is plenty of sunlight, you can place them there and bring them back into the kitchen when needed.

*Bloom and Harvest*

You can begin harvesting your basil as early as 60 days from planting – that is if you started them from seeds. You will know that your basil is mature when it grows up to 3 feet tall. But you can actually begin harvesting some leaves when they reach 6 inches in height. You don't have to wait until your basil reaches full maturity. However, do note that there is a type of basil that grows up to 6 feet tall when it matures (i.e. sweet basil).

You basically want to harvest the top leaves. Pinch off bunches of leaves from the top of the plant. This will prevent it from blooming. When basil blooms the leaves begin to lose flavor. Don't worry, the flowers are edible too. However, most Italian dishes require basil leaves not basil flowers. When your basil blooms it will soon start to produce seeds, which you can plant for the next generation of basil herb plants.

*Basil Growing Tips*

If you love Italian food then you ought to grow some tomatoes as well. The good news is that basil and tomatoes usually end up as nice neighbors to each other. So, you can have a row of basil pots standing side by side with a row of tomatoes. Both types of plants actually help each other grow.

Basil plants are best grown in 12 inch pots. They will require that much space for their roots. These herbs really love the heat and will be grown easier during the warmer months. Once the temperature hits 70 degrees Fahrenheit (the ideal temperature at night for these plants is around 50 degrees Fahrenheit) you can start planting your next batch of basil. Remember that you can start your seeds about a month before the last frost of spring (check the weather report often).

Basil loves nutrient rich soil so pick your garden soil carefully. These plants also don't like dry ground, so keep the soil moist. If you're growing a row of basil then you should space them 10 inches apart so they have enough room to stretch out.

Watch out for aphids, these are the most common pests that infest basil. Slugs and beetles also can become a problem for these plants.

**How to Grow Thyme at Home**

Thyme is a Mediterranean herb and it's also very aromatic. These herbs love the sunlight and prefer dryer living conditions. Thyme improves the flavors of other food like tomatoes and garlic. Thyme is also a medicinal herb and is known to have antiseptic properties. Thyme can also be used to preserve meat. Some manufacturers also use thyme to manufacture certain types of perfumes and scents.

Thyme is best grown in the parts of your home where there is full sun. These herbs grow best in areas with USDA hardiness of 5 to 9+.

*When to Harvest Thyme*

Thyme is a woody perennial. They usually don't grow that tall; only about 6 to 10 inches in height. If you grow a bunch of them they will usually grow to about the same height. Note that these herbs are extremely aromatic. You can actually smell them when grown indoors in the kitchen.

Once your thyme is established in your garden you can begin to harvest them any time. You're going to need a pair of scissors to cut off a few stems. The flowers are edible especially when they are still fresh blossoms. Note that the flowers attract bees very well.

*Which Type of Thyme to Grow*

Note that there are more than 300 species of thyme. The lemon scented thyme specie is popular for use in kitchens. These are the ones that have patches of gold colors on their leaves. They usually have a minty and lemony taste.

If you're looking for herbs that you can use to add a carpet of green on your lawn, then you can grow some woody thyme. They are odorless, which means they have no scent at all. Other thyme variants add refreshing aromas to the environment. There are species of thyme that smell of rose and lavender. There are also species that smell of oranges. Pick the type of thyme according to your needs.

*Tips for Growing Thyme*

When thyme is grown in areas with warmer climates they tend to grow shrubby. Prune them hard so they don't get too woody. Remove any parts that have died out. Pruning can begin in early spring. You can also prune them after they have flowered.

If you're growing lots of thyme, make sure to space the plants 6 inches apart. Notice that they will cover their individual areas. Note that thyme also grows very well indoors. However, you should place them near windows so they can get as much sunlight as needed.

Make sure to choose lean soil for thyme. These plants will not require a lot of moisture. Too much watering will eventually cause this herb to rot. Ensure proper drainage when growing them indoors, especially during the winter months. You don't need to water them as often as the other plants and herbs.

Ants are the most common problems for thyme especially when you grow them outdoors. These little pests tend to make their nests where your thyme plants grow. When these pests nest in where the thyme plants grow, they disrupt the plant root system, which eventually kills the plants.

**Growing Your Own Culinary Oregano**

Oregano is a signature herb for many cuisines. If you like Mexican food, Italian food, and Spanish food you'll notice that they have one thing in common – many of their dishes make use of oregano. Most consumers buy oregano in bottles or other packaging. They're usually sold in dried form but they really taste better when they're plucked off the plant fresh.

They're very easy to grow, which makes them another ideal herb to add to any home garden. Some oregano variants can be grown successfully indoors but most of the time they won't get enough sun indoors. Some people use oregano as perennial ground covers. Note that some oregano variants tend to get woody, so you should pick the species that suits your needs.

The most common specie of oregano is the Greek variant. You may have heard of the Mexican oregano, which is usually part of many chili powder recipes. FYI – the Mexican variant is not true oregano. If you're looking for an ornamental plant then the golden oregano is your best bet; it's the one that doesn't have a scent.

*Sun Exposure*

Most oregano breeds need a lot of sun. In fact, you should place them on the spot of your garden that has the longest exposure to sunlight. Oregano is best grown within Hardiness Zones 5 up to Zone 10 (depending on the oregano species).

*Harvesting Oregano*

Oregano usually begin as plants that stay on the ground. However, as they mature they grow up to 2 feet tall (some variants can grow taller). You can actually begin harvesting oregano leaves even before they become fully mature.

*Garden Placement*

Some gardeners use oregano as edging plants, which will make your garden plot look neat. Remember that these herbs require very little maintenance and they're very hardy. Oregano also works as great ground cover, so you can use them to fill any unused area in your yard.

*Which Oregano Variant to Plant*

There are two types of oregano that are generally used in cooking as well as in medicinal treatments. The most common one is Greek oregano, which has the scent that everyone is familiar with. The other popular variant is called common oregano, which isn't as aromatic. In fact, it even tastes sweet and is popular in both English and French cuisine.

*More Oregano Growing Tips*

Trim your oregano all the way to its soil. This will encourage the plant to grow more stems. Older stems tend to get woody so you should snip those off completely.

Make sure that you plant your oregano in well-drained soil. If you use rich soil then expect the herb to produce less essential oils and it won't have the usual smell. The current climate conditions have a direct effect on the taste and flavor that oregano can produce. Make sure to maintain optimal growing conditions. Temperatures should remain above 45 degrees Fahrenheit (remember that this is a Mediterranean herb).

To prevent these herbs from turning too bushy, pinch off the flowers on the spot. This will also prevent them from seeding. Allow these herbs to grow seeds only when you intend to make new starts. These herbs don't tolerate winter temperatures that well, so you should grow your oregano seeds before the change of seasons.

## Growing Your Parsley at Home

Parsley is one of the herbs you can grow indoors and outdoors. If you grow them indoors you can protect them from frozen winters. This also means that you can have fresh parsley all year round.

Parsley is known for its unique flavor. Other than making your dishes taste great, parsley also has a lot of medicinal uses. Herbalists often use it to treat digestive problems. It is also used to lower blood pressure. Parsley is full of vitamins and minerals. It is rich vitamin c, iron, and calcium.

*Harvesting Parsley*

Parsley is best served fresh. Frozen or dried parsley is good but you don't get as much flavor from this herb when they're preserved. Fresh parsley has all the rich flavors that you're looking for.

When you harvest parsley, remember that you can cut all the way to the stems. But make sure to leave at least a couple of inches of stem to encourage the plant to grow more. Parsley leaves and stems are used in different cuisines. The newer leaves and stems tend to have more flavor.

*Sunlight Exposure*

Parsley is also a Mediterranean herb, which means that you should try to provide the same living conditions for them as oregano, so that they will grow optimally. This means that these herbs require at least 6 hours of direct sunlight each day. If you're growing parsley (or any Mediterranean herb) indoors, ensure that they have a lot of sun or artificial light.

If you're using artificial light (e.g. during cold winter months) then you should keep the light source around 6 inches away (preferably above them) from your herbs. Since the light is artificial, leave it on for 14 hours each day.

*More Growing Tips for Parsley*

Parsley can grow up to 30 centimeters tall (about one foot tall). Leave them under the sun all day and they will remain bright and green. Don't forget to turn the plant or else it will lean in the direction of the light source.

Parsley plants prefer evenly moist soil. So make sure that the pot and soil you're using has enough drainage. These herbs prefer temperature ranges of 60 to 75 degrees Fahrenheit. They're not picky about the type of soil you plant them in, but make sure the soil is of good quality.

Remember to use a balanced fertilizer for your parsley, especially if you're growing them indoors. Note that parsley seeds germinate slowly. They may even take up to 3 weeks before they begin to sprout. You can speed up the growing process by soaking the seeds in warm water and then leave them there overnight. After that, you can plant them in your seed bed the following morning.

**Raising Rosemary**

Here are some tips for when you raise rosemary (pun intended). The Latin name of this herb literally means "The Sea's Dew." Rosemary is used in many Mediterranean dishes. Other than being used for culinary purposes, this herb is also ornamental. Compared to some of the other herbs already mentioned here, this one is rather low maintenance. It will grow quite well without a lot of human intervention.

*Tips for Growing Rosemary*

Unless you're really experienced with growing herbs, it isn't recommended that you grow rosemary herbs from seeds. It can be really frustrating and it will require a lot of trial and error. Even when you successfully grow one from seeds, the new sprouts may always not live up to the splendor of their ancestors.

The easiest and most practical way to raise rosemary shrubs is to get a full grown one from the nursery. You can always let the experts at the nursery do the heavy lifting. They usually propagate rosemary seedlings using cuttings. You can give it a few tries and grow your rosemary from cuttings as well.

Take off a cutting from a mature rosemary plant that is about a couple of inches long. Get one that is a new offshoot from the ground. Remove the leaves on the bottom half of the shoot and then dip it in a small amount of rooting hormone; which you can buy from any garden supplier.

Fill a pot with or container with well-draining starting mix. A potting mix for starts that has peat moss in it will be a good option. Stick your rosemary cutting into the pot with the end that was dipped in rooting hormone going into the soil. Be careful not to break your piece of rosemary when you put it into the soil mix.

Remember to spray water on the soil so it doesn't dry up. The container or pot should be placed in an area with indirect sunlight. Keep watering for two or three weeks. After three weeks test the rosemary cutting to see if it has grown roots. To do that, gently tug on the cuttings to see if they show resistance.

Once roots have grown, transplant the new rosemary into new individual containers. Their permanent home should have a diameter of about four inches. Once transplanted, you should pinch off a small piece from the top of the cutting to encourage the new plant to start growing branches. It is recommended that you grow your rosemary in containers.

*Light Exposure*

Rosemary isn't hardy enough to overcome any winter outdoors. Once the temperature dips around the 30's you should bring these herbs indoors. Rosemary herbs require a lot of sunlight, so keep them where the sun touches your garden. If you're growing them indoors then place them near windows. These herbs require around 6 to 8 hours of sunlight.

*Pests and Possible Problems*

Rosemary is susceptible to powdery mildew even when it is kept indoors. It doesn't kill the herb but it weakens it. To prevent mildew from forming, make sure to allow the pot soil dry out in between your watering schedule. Keeping the herbs in direct sunlight will also help to prevent mildew and fungus formation. Another trick is to turn the fan on your herbs. This helps create a small breeze that will blow the mildew away. You can turn the fan on a few hours each day.

Rosemary is also prone to both spider mites and aphids. The only way to get rid of these is to get down and dirty with them and remove them on sight. You can spray some mild insecticidal soap but only when you have an infestation. Remember that you're going to eat the said herbs and you don't want to have any type of pesticide on your food. Make sure to follow all package instructions religiously.

*Moving to a Bigger Pot*

There will come a time in a rosemary herb's life when it has to move to a bigger pot. This actually happens to almost all plants, especially when you're dealing with herbs. If you find that it has grown so much and that it's not getting enough water (some leaves are pale and/or dying) then it's time to transfer it to a larger container.

Once you have transferred the herb, allow the plant to recuperate. Replanting it will cause a lot of stress.

Of course you still want to manage the size of your rosemary plant (or any herb for that matter). Keep trimming the top after moving your plant to a new pot. Don't forget to root, prune, and trim off two inches off the sides as well as on the bottom so that your herb doesn't grow too big.

**The Sage**

People usually add sage to their recipes to add that distinct earthy freshness. These evergreen shrubs are staples in some kitchens. Although there are different types of sage plants, everyone just call them either common sage or garden sage. Note that there are ornamental breeds of sage. However, the common sage, the one that is used in the kitchen is a lot hardier. Sage thrives in areas that are classed as USDA hardiness zone 5 all the way to 9.

You can grow your sage from transplants, root cuttings, and seeds. You can also get starts and young sage plants to make things a lot easier. Remember to keep the soil well drained.

*Sunlight Exposure*

Sage grows very well under full sun. In places that have a warmer climate, you should give them some sun time in the afternoon when it's not too hot. Make sure to avoid keeping sage leaves damp and wet for prolonged periods of time. Giving them around 6 hours of sunlight will be best.

*Harvesting Sage*

A full grown sage plant will be 2 feet tall. It's also going to be around 3 feet wide. They do tend to sprawl across rather than reach high to the sky. Don't harvest anything from your sage herb for the first year. After the year is over you can harvest anytime you want. Your plant will stay with you and will live up to 4 years before needing a replacement.

*Pests and Problems*

The good thing about sage is that it is really hardy and insects seldom bother it. You can grow your sage beside other herbs to help drive insects away. The biggest sage killer is excess watering.

# Chapter 4 – Getting Rid of Pests Naturally

In the previous chapter, it was mentioned that sage naturally repels insects and other pests. It will be beneficial to place your sage beside other plants to serve as natural protection. Apart from doing this, there are many other ways to get rid of pests naturally without using pesticides.

The following are some natural pest control tips you should know

- Not all insects are pests. Some insects are actually beneficial (e.g. praying mantis, hover flies, lacewings, lady bugs, and ichneumon wasps). Some insects even help herbs pollinate. Identify the type of insect first before you decide to use any type of pest control
- Prevention is always the better option. Pull any weak plants and isolate them until they are better. Use only organic and healthy soil. Clear any area that has debris and weeds where insects can breed.
- If you have to use mulch, use clean mulch
- Don't allow the leaves of your herbs to remain wet too long. This will help prevent the formation of fungus.

- Make sure to clean your tools in case you have used them on an infected plant.
- Interplant resilient herbs with the ones that grow well with them.
- Spray plants with fungus infections with water and two tablespoons of baking soda.
- Spray plants with powdery mildew with a mix of water and milk.
- Sprinkle some diatomaceous earth on plants that have been infested by snails, slugs, and other harmful insects.
- Another simple non-toxic spray solution is a combination of water (1 quart), cayenne pepper, and a few drops of mild bath soap. Let the mixture stand overnight before spraying. Make sure to shake the container before you spray. This mixture is effective on insects and mites.
- Use traps and barriers.

There are other natural methods of pest control. You can ask your local garden supplier about them. If none of them work after you've tried everything then it's time to pull out the big guns and use pesticides. Use pesticides that are designed for edible plants and use sparingly or only when needed.

# Conclusion

Thank you again for downloading this book!

I hope this book was able to help you learn more about herb gardening!

The next step is to put this information to use, and begin working on your very own herb garden!

Finally, if you enjoyed this book, please take the time to share your thoughts and post a review on Amazon. It'd be greatly appreciated!

Thank you and good luck!